...rnationally successful film by Steven Spielberg.

She has published three other volumes of poetry, which have all been published by The Women's Press: *Horses Make a Landscape Look More Beautiful* (1985), *Good Night, Willie Lee, I'll See You in the Morning* (1987) and *Revolutionary Petunias* (1988); and two collections of prose writing: *In Search of Our Mothers' Gardens: Womanist Prose* (The Women's Press, 1984), and *Living by the Word* (The Women's Press, 1988). She has written two collections of short stories: *In Love and Trouble* (The Women's Press, 1984) and *You Can't Keep a Good Woman Down* (The Women's Press, 1982). Her five novels are *The Color Purple*; *The Temple of My Familiar* (The Women's Press, 1989), which appeared in the *New York Times* bestseller list for four months; *The Third Life of Grange Copeland* (The Women's Press, 1985); *Meridian* (The Women's Press, 1982), of which CLR James said 'I have not read a novel superior to this'; and *Possessing the Secret of Joy* (1992).

Alice Walker's complete poetry is now collected together in *Her Blue Body Everything We Know: Earthling Poems 1965–1990 Complete*, and her complete short stories appear in *The Complete Stories*, both published by The Women's Press.

Also by Alice Walker from The Women's Press:

Fiction and poetry

Meridian
The Color Purple
The Color Purple: Special 10th Anniversary Limited Edition
In Love and Trouble
Horses Make a Landscape Look More Beautiful
The Third Life of Grange Copeland
Good Night, Willie Lee, I'll See You in the Morning
Revolutionary Petunias
The Temple of My Familiar
Her Blue Body Everything We Know: Earthling Poems 1965–1990
Complete
The Complete Stories

Essays

In Search of Our Mothers' Gardens: Womanist Prose
Living by the Word: Selected Writings 1973–1987

ONCE

Alice Walker

Published in Great Britain by The Women's Press Ltd, 1986
A member of the Namara Group
34 Great Sutton Street, London EC1V 0DX

Reprinted 1987, 1995

First published in the United States of America by Harcourt Brace
Jovanovich, 1976

British Library Cataloguing-in-Publication Data
Walker, Alice, 1944–
    Once.
    I. Title
    811'.54 PS3573.A425

ISBN 0 7043 4030 5

Printed and bound in Great Britain by BPC Paperbacks Ltd, Aylesbury,
Bucks

For Howard Zinn

Poverty was not a calamity for me. It was always balanced by the richness of light . . . circumstances helped me. To correct a natural indifference I was placed half-way between misery and the sun. Misery kept me from believing that all was well under the sun, and the sun taught me that history wasn't everything.

—Albert Camus, *De l'envers et l'endroit*

CONTENTS

ONCE

AFRICAN IMAGES

Glimpses from a Tiger's Back

i

Beads around
my neck
Mt. Kenya away
over pineappled hills
Kikuyuland.

ii

A book of poems
Mt. Kenya's
Bluish peaks
"Wangari!"*
My new name.

iii

A green copse
And hovering
Quivering
Near our bus
A shy gazelle.

* Kikuyu clan name indicating honorary acceptance into the Leopard clan.

iv

morning mists
On the road
an Elephant
He knows
his rights.

v

A strange noise!
"Perhaps an elephant
is eating our roof"
In the morning
much blue.

vi

A tall warrior
and at his feet
only
Elephant bones.

vii

Elephant legs
In a store
To hold
Umbrellas.

viii

A young man
Puts a question
In his language
I invariably
End up
Married.

ix

The clear Nile
A fat crocodile
Scratches his belly
And yawns.

x

The rain forest
Red orchids—glorious!
And near one's eyes
The spinning cobra.

xi

A small boat
A placid lake
Suddenly at one's hand
Two ears—
Hippopotamus.

xii

An ocean of grass
A sea of sunshine
And near my hand
Water buffalo.

xiii

See! through the trees!
A leopard in
the branches—
No, only a giraffe
Munching his dinner.

xiv

Fast rapids
Far below
Begins
The lazy Nile.

xv

A silent lake
Bone strewn banks
Luminous
In the sun.

xvi

Uganda mountains
Black soil
White snow
And in the valley
Zebra.

xvii

African mornings
Are not for sleeping
In the early noon
The servant comes
To wake me.

xviii

Very American
I want to eat
The native food—
But a whole goat!

xix

Holding three fingers
The African child
Looked up at me
The sky was very
Blue.

8

xx

In the dance
I see a girl
Go limp
"It is a tactic"
I think.

xxi

"America!?"   "Yes."
"But you are like
my aunt's cousin
who married so-and-so."
"Yes, (I say), I know."

xxii

On my knees
The earringed lady
Thinks I'm praying
She drops her sisal
and runs.

xxiii

"You are a Negro?"
        "Yes"
"But that is a kind
of food—isn't it—
the white man used to

eat you???"
      "Well—"

xxiv

Unusual things amuse us
A little African girl
Sees my white friend
And runs
She thinks he wants her
For his dinner.

xxv

The fresh corpse
Of a white rhinoceros
His horn gone
Some Indian woman
Will be approached
Tonight.

xxvi

The man in the
Scarlet shirt
Wanted to talk
but had no words—
I had words
but no Scarlet
Shirt.

xxvii

floating shakily down the
nile
on my rented raft
I try to be a native
queen
a prudent giraffe
on the bank
turns up
          his nose.

xxviii

We eat Metoke*
with three fingers—
other things
get two fingers
and one of those
a thumb.

xxix

That you loved me
I felt sure
Twice you asked
me gently
if I liked the
strange

* *A food staple of the Buganda*
in Uganda, made from plantains.

gray
stew.

xxx

Pinching both my legs
the old man kneels
before me on the
ground
his head white
Ah! Africa's mountain
peaks
Snow to grace
eternal spring!

xxxi

To build a hut
One needs mud
and sisal
And friendly
Neighbors.

xxxii

Where the glacier was
A lake
Where the lake is
Sunshine
And redheaded
Marabou storks.

xxxiii

On a grumpy day
An African child
Chants "good morning"
—I have never seen
Such bright sun!

xxxiv

The Nairobi streets
At midnight
Deserted
The hot dog man
Folds up his cart.

xxxv

In Nairobi
I pestered an
Indian boy to
Sell me a
Hat
For five shillings—
How bright
His eyes were!

xxxvi

In a kunzu
Long and white

Stands my African
Dad
The sound of drums
Fills
The air!

xxxvii

On my brother's motorcycle
The Indian mosques
And shops fade behind us
My hair takes flight
He laughs
He has not seen such hair
Before.

xxxviii

An African girl
Gives me a pineapple
Her country's national
Flower
How proudly she
Blinks the eye
Put out
By a sharp pineapple
Frond.
I wonder if I should
Kneel
At her bare little
Feet?

xxxix

At first night
I sat alone
& watched the
      sun set
behind
   the
aberdares
  During
    the day
      my legs
and the sun
  belonged
    to
  the village
    children.

xl

Under the moon
luminous
huts. . . .
Brown breasts stuck
out to taunt
the sullen wind.

xli

A crumbling
hut . . .

in the third
room
a red chenille
bedspread
(by Cannon)
a cracked
jar
of violet
    lilies
      (by?)

xlii

The native women
thought me
strange
until they
saw me follow you
to your hut.

xliii

In Kampala
the young king
goes often
to Church
the young girls here
are
So pious.

xliv

Settled behind
tall banana trees
the little hut
is overcovered by
their leaves
patiently it waits
for autumn
which never comes. . . .

xlv

in my journal
I thought I could
capture
everything. . . .
Listen!
the soft wings of cranes
sifting the salt sea
air.

LOVE

i

A dark stranger
My heart searches
Him out
"Papa!"

ii

An old man in white
Calls me "mama"
It does not take much
To know
He wants me for
His wife—
He has no teeth
But is kind.

iii

The American from
Minnesota
Speaks Harvardly
of Revolution—
Men of the Mau Mau
Smile
Their fists holding
Bits of
Kenya earth.

iv

A tall Ethiopian
Grins at me
The grass burns
My bare feet.

v

Drums outside
My window
Morning whirls
In
I have danced all
Night.

vi

The bearded Briton
Wears a shirt of
Kenya flags
I am at home
He says.

vii

Down the hill
A grove of trees
And on this spot
The magic tree.

viii

The Kenya air!
Miles of hills
Mountains
And holding both
My hands
A Mau Mau leader.

ix

And in the hut
The only picture—
Of Jesus

x

Explain to the
Women
In the village
That you are
Twenty
And belong—
To no one.

KARAMOJANS

i

A tall man
Without clothes
Beautiful
Like a statue
Up close
His eyes
Are running
Sores.

ii

The Noble Savage
Erect
No shoes on his
feet
His pierced ears
Infected.

iii

"Quite incredible—
your hair-do is
most divine——
Held together
With *cow* dung?
You mean——?!

The lady stares
At her fingers.

iv

A proper English meal
Near the mountains
"More tea, please"
Down the street
A man walks
Quite completely
Nude.

v

Bare breasts loose
In the sun
The skin cracked
The nipples covered
With flies
But she is an old
Woman
What?—twenty?

vi

A Catholic church
The chaste cross
Stark
Against the purple sky.

We surprise a
couple there alone
In prayer?

vii

There is no need for
Sadness
After the dying boy
There is the living girl
Who throws you a
kiss.

viii

How bright the little
girl's
Eyes were!
a first sign of
Glaucoma.

ix

The Karamojans
Never civilized
A proud people
I think there
Are
A hundred left.

ONCE

i

Green lawn
a picket fence
flowers—
My friend smiles
she had heard
that Southern
jails
were drab.

Looking up I see
a strong arm
raised
the Law
Someone in America
is being
protected
            (from me.)

In the morning
there was
a man in grey
but the sky
was blue.

ii

"Look at that
nigger with those
white folks!"
        My dark
Arrogant friend
turns calmly, curiously
helpfully,
            "Where?" he
                asks.

It was the fifth
arrest
In as many
    days
How glad I am
that I can
look
surprised
            still.

iii

Running down
Atlanta
            streets
With my sign
I see heads
        turn
Eyes

        goggle
"a nice girl
   like her!"

A Negro cook
assures
          her mistress—

But I had seen
the fingers
near her eyes
   wet with
      tears.

iv

One day in
Georgia
Working around
the Negro section
My friend got a
letter
in
the mail
—the letter
said
      "I hope you're
having a good
time
fucking all
      the niggers."

"Sweet," I winced.
          "Who
              wrote it?"

"mother."
          she
              said.

That day she sat
          a long time
a little black girl
in pigtails
on her lap

Her eyes were very
Quiet.

She used to tell the big colored ladies
her light eyes just
the same
"I am alone
my mother died."
Though no other
letter
came.

v

It is true—
I've always loved

the daring
          ones
Like the black young
man
Who tried
to crash
All barriers
at once,
      wanted to
swim
At a white
beach (in Alabama)
Nude.

vi

Peter always
thought
the only
way to
"enlighten"
southern towns
was to
introduce
      himself
to
the county
sheriff
      first thing.

Another thing
Peter wanted—
was to be
cremated
    but we
couldn't
    find him
when he needed it.

But he was just a yid
    seventeen.

    vii

    I
never liked
white folks
    really
    it
happened quite
  suddenly
    one
    day
A pair of
  amber
  eyes
    I
  think
  he
  had.

viii

I *don't* think
   integration
      entered
         into it
            officer.

You see
   there was
      this little
         Negro
           girl
Standing here
    alone
    and her
        mother
           went into
    that store
        there

then—
    there came by
this little boy
   here
without his
   mother
& eating
   an
ice cream cone
—see there it is—
   strawberry

Anyhow

      and the little
        girl was
        hungry
        and
        stronger
        than
        the little
        boy—

Who is too
    fat
  really,

       anyway.

ix

Someone said
     to
        me
that
    if
       the South
rises
    again
it will do so
  "from
the grave."

Someone
       else
           said
if the South
  rises
      again
he would
      "step on
        it."

Dick Gregory
  said that
    if the
      South
        rises
      again
      there is
      a
      secret
      plan.

But I say—
  if the
      South
rises
     again
It will not
  do
    so
in my presence.

x

"but I don'
really
    give a fuck
Who
  my daughter
      marries—"
the lady
was
adorable—
it was in a
tavern
i remember
her daughter
sat there
beside her
tugging
at
her arm
sixteen—
very shy
            and
very pim
        pled.

xi

then there
was
the charming
      half-wit

who told
the judge
re: indecent exposure
"but when I
step out
  of the
  tub
I look
  Good—
just because
my skin
is black
don't mean
it ain't
pretty
            you old bastard!)
what will we
finally do
with
prejudice

some people like
to take a walk
after a bath.

xii

"look, honey
said
the
blond

amply
boobed
babe
in the
green
 g
string

"i like you
sure
i ain't
prejudiced

but the
lord didn't
give me
legs
like
these
because
he
wanted
to see'm
dangling
from a
poplar!"

"But they're so
      much
            prettier
                  than mine.

Would you really mind?"
he asked
wanting her to dance.

xiii

I remember
seeing
a little girl,
dreaming—perhaps,
  hit by
    a
  van truck

"That nigger was
in the way!" the
man
      said
      to
understanding cops.

        But was she?
          She was
            just eight
              her mother
                said
          and little
                for
              her age.

xiv

then there was
the
picture of
the
bleak-eyed
little black
girl
waving the
american
flag
holding it
gingerly
with
the very
tips
of her
fingers.

CHIC FREEDOM'S

REFLECTION

(for Marilyn Pryce)

One day
Marilyn marched
beside me (demon-
stration)
and we ended up
at county farm
no phone
no bail
something about
"traffic vio-
lation"
which irrelevance
Marilyn dismissed
with a shrug
    She
had just got
    back
from
    Paris France
        In
      the
    Alabama
      hell
    she

      smell-
          ed
    so
   wonderful
like spring
& love
    &
freedom

    She
   wore a
SNCC pin
right between
  her breasts
   near her
     heart
& with a chic
  (on "jail?")
accent
  & nod of
condescent
  to frumpy
   work-house
     hags
powdered her nose
    tip-
        toe
in a badge.

SOUTH:

THE NAME OF HOME

i

all that night
I prayed for eyes to see again
whose last sight
had been
a broken bottle
held negligently
in a racist
fist
God give us trees to plant
and hands and eyes to
love them.

ii

When I am here again
the years of ease between
fall away
The smell of one
magnolia
sends my heart running
through the swamps.

iii

the earth is red
here—
the trees bent, weeping
what secrets will not
the ravished land
reveal
of its abuse?

iv

an old mistress
of my mother's
gives me
bloomers for christmas
ten sizes
too big
her intentions are
good my father
says
but typical—
neither the color
she knows
nor the
    number.

HYMN

I well remember
A time when
"Amazing Grace" was
All the rage
In the South.
'Happy' black mothers arguing
Agreement with
Illiterate sweating preachers
Hemming and hawing blessedness
Meekness
Inheritance of earth, e.g.,
Mississippi cotton fields?

And in the North
Roy Hamilton singing
"What is America to me?"
Such a good question
From a nice slum
In North Philly.

My God! the songs and
The people and the lives
Started here—
Weaned on 'happy' tears
Black fingers clutching black teats
On black Baptist benches—
Some mother's troubles that everybody's
Seen
And nobody wants to see.

I can remember the rocking of
The church
And embarrassment
At my mother's shouts
Like it was all—'her happiness'—
Going to kill her.
My father's snores
Punctuating eulogies
His loud singing
Into fluffy grey caskets
A sleepy tear
In his eye.

Amazing Grace
How sweet the sound
That saved a wretch
Like me
I once was lost
But now I'm found
Was blind
But now
I see.

Mahalia Jackson, Clara Ward, Fats Waller,
Ray Charles,
Sitting here embarrassed with me
Watching the birth
Hearing the cries
Bearing witness
To the child,
Music.

THE DEMOCRATIC ORDER:

SUCH THINGS IN TWENTY YEARS

I UNDERSTOOD

My father
(back blistered)
beat me
because I
could not
stop crying.
He'd had
enough 'fuss'
he said
for one damn
voting day.

THEY WHO FEEL DEATH

(for martyrs)

They who feel death close as a breath
Speak loudly in unlighted rooms
Lounge upright in articulate gesture
Before the herd of jealous Gods

Fate finds them receiving
At home.

Grim the warrior forest who present
Casual silence with casual battle cries
Or stand unflinchingly lodged

In common sand
Crucified.

ON BEING ASKED TO LEAVE

A PLACE OF HONOR FOR ONE

OF COMFORT; PREFERABLY

IN THE NORTHERN

SUBURBS

*(for those who work and stay in the
ragged Mississippis of the world)*

In this place of helmets and tar
the anxious burblings of recreants
buzz over us
we bent laughing to oars of gold

We regard them as Antigone her living kin

Fat chested pigeons
resplendent of prodigious riches
reaped in body weight
taking bewildered pecks
at eagles
as though *muck*
were God.

THE ENEMY

in gray, scarred Leningrad
a tiny fist unsnapped to show
crumpled heads
of pink and yellow flowers
snatched hurriedly on the go
in the cold spring shower—

consent or not
countries choose
cold or hot
win or lose
to speak of wars
yellow and red
but there is much
let it be said
for children.

COMPULSORY

CHAPEL

i

A quiet afternoon
the speaker
dull
the New Testament
washed out
Through the window
a lonely
      blue-jay
makes noisy song.

ii

The speaker crashes
on
through his speech
All eyes are
upon him
Over his left
ear
the thick hair
is beginning
to slip.

iii

I would not mind
    if I were

                a sinner,

but as it is
—let me assure you—
I sleep alone.

TO THE MAN

IN THE YELLOW TERRY

Dawn came at six today
Held back by hope
A lost cause—
Melted like snow
In the middle of
The day.

The sun shines clear fire
The earth once more
Like it was—
Old promises
Rise up
(Our honored
    Ghosts)
And the lonely truths
Of love
Pledged.

Here we lie
You and I—
Your mind, unaccountable,
My mind simply
Stopped—
Like a clock struck
By the treachery
Of time.

The sky blue, empty,
Unfathomable—
As I am.
Look at it brighten
And fill and
Astonish
With each movement
Of your
Eyes.

The wren who does not
Sing
I take my simple
Flight
Silent, unmetaphoric
Dressed in brown
I say
Good-bye.

Will you think it funny
Later on
To find you had
Almost
Given shelter
To a
Thief?

THE KISS

i was kissed once
by a beautiful man
all blond and
              czech
riding through bratislava
on a motor bike
screeching "don't yew let me fall off heah naow!"

the funny part was
he spoke english
and setting me gallantly
on my feet
kissed me for
not anyhow *looking*
like aunt jemima.

WHAT OVID

TAUGHT ME

What does it matter? you ask
　　If protocol
　　　　falls
　　　After artichokes
　　　　and steak,
　　　　　Vivaldi
　　　　　　and
　　　　　　No
　　　　　　Wine

For God's sake
Let's not be traditional!

　　　　　But I,
　　　　Unused bed
　　　　　All tousled
　　　Sing nursery rhymes
　　　　　Chant
　　　　　　Strange
　　　　　　　Chants

　　　Count stray insects
　　　On the ceiling
　　　　and
　　　　Wonder—

Why don't you shut up and

　　　　　　　get in?

MORNINGS / *of an impossible love*

On the morning you woke beside me—already thinking of going away—the sun did not fill my window as it does most mornings. Instead there was cloud and threat of snow. How I wish it could always be this way—that on mornings he cannot come himself, the sun might send me you.

Watching you frown at your face in the mirror this
morning I almost thought you disapproved of the little
dark shadow standing behind you its arms around your
waist. . . .

Two mornings ago you left my little house. Only two
steps from my fingers & you were gone, swallowed down
swiftly by my spiral stairs. . . .

Why do you wish to give me over to someone else? "Such and such young man you're sure to like" you say "for he is a fine, cheerful fellow, very sensitive" and one thing and another. Sometimes it is as if you'd never listened to my heartbeat, never heard my breathing in your ear, never seen my eyes when you say such things. . . .

This is what you told me once. Must I believe you? "We are really Easterners, you and I. The rising of the Sun brings with it our whole Philosophy."

SO WE'VE COME

AT LAST

TO FREUD

Do not hold my few years
                        against me
In my life, childhood
                was a myth
So long ago it seemed, even
                        in the cradle.

Don't label my love with slogans;
My father can't be blamed
                        for my affection
Or lack of it;
ask him.
He won't understand you.

Don't sit on holy stones
                        as you,
Loving me
            and hating me, condemn.
There is no need for that.

I like to think that I, though
                        young it's true,
Know what
            I'm doing.

That I, once unhappy, am
Now
Quite sanely
                    jubilant,
& that neither you
Nor I can
Deny
That no matter how
"Sick"
The basis
is
Of what we have,
What we *do* have
Is Good.

JOHANN

You look at me with children
In your eyes,
  Blond, blue-eyed
Teutons
Charmingly veiled
In bronze
  Got from me.

What would Hitler say?

I am brown-er
Than a jew
Being one step
Beyond that Colored scene.
You are the Golden Boy,
Shiny but bloody
And with that ancient martial tune
Only your heart is out of step—
You love.

But even knowing love
I shrink from you. Blond
And Black; it is too charged a combination.
Charged with past and present wars,
Charged with frenzy
and with blood

Dare I kiss your German mouth?
Touch the perfect muscles
Underneath the yellow shirt
Blending coolly
With your yellow
Hair?

I shudder at the whiteness
Of your hands.

Blue is too cold a color
For eyes.

But white, I think, is the color
Of honest flowers,

And blue is the color
Of the sky.

Come closer then and hold out to me
Your white and faintly bloodied hands.
I will kiss your German mouth
And will touch the helpless
White skin, gone red,
Beneath the yellow shirt.
I will rock the yellow head against
My breast, brown and yielding.

But I tell you, love,
There is still much to fear.
We have only seen the

First of wars
First of frenzies
First of blood.

Someday, perhaps, we will be
Made to learn
That blond and black
Cannot love.

But until that rushing day
I will not reject you.
I will kiss your fearful
German mouth.
And you—
Look at me boldly
With surging, brown-blond teutons
In your eyes.

THE SMELL

OF LEBANON

in balmy
  iconic
prague
I offered
my bosom
    to a wandering arab student
who spoke
much
of
Lebanon
    and
      his father's
        orchards

          it
        was near
        a castle
        near
        a river
        near
        the sun
        and
        warm

&
where he
bent
and kissed
  me
on the swelling
brown
smelled for
a short
     lingering
        time
of
  apples.

WARNING

To love a man wholly
love him
feet first
    head down
    eyes cold
    closed
in depression.

It is too easy to love
a surfer
white eyes
godliness &
        bronze
in the bright sun.

THE BLACK PRINCE

Very proud
he barely asked directions
to a nearby
hotel
    but no
    tired-eyed
    little village chief
    should spend his
    first night
    in chilly London
    alone.

MEDICINE

Grandma sleeps with
my sick
            grand-
pa so she
can get him
during the night
medicine
to stop
   the pain

   In
the morning
   clumsily
      I
   wake
      them

Her eyes
look at me
from under-
            neath
his withered
arm

The
medicine
is all
in
her long
un-
braided
hair.

BALLAD OF

THE BROWN GIRL

i've got two
hundred
        dollars
the girl said
on her head
she wore a
school cap
—blue—
& brown she
looked no
more than
ten
but a freshman in
college?
well, hard
to tell—

i'll give you
'three hundred'
'fo' hunna'
'five wads of jack'

but "*mrs.* whatsyourname . . ."
the doctor says
with impatiently tolerant
eyes

you should *want*
it
you know . . .
talk it over with
your folks
you *may be*
         surprised. . . .

the next morning
her slender
neck broken
her note short
and of cryptic
collegiate
make—

     just

"Question—

did ever brown
daughter to black
father a white
baby
    take—?"

SUICIDE

First, suicide notes should be
(not long) but written
second,
all suicide notes
should be signed
in blood
by hand
and to the point—
that point being, perhaps,
that there is none.
Thirdly, if it is the thought
of rest that
fascinates
laziness should be admitted
in the clearest terms.
Then, all things done
ask those outraged
consider their happiest
summer
& tell if the days it
adds up to
is one.

EXCUSE

Tonight it is the wine (or not the wine)
or a letter from you (or not a letter from you)
I sit
listen to the complacency of the rain
write a poem, kill myself there

It brings less pain—

Tonight it rains, tomorrow will be bright
tomorrow I'll say "yesterday was the same
only the rain . . .

and my shoes too tight."

TO DIE

BEFORE ONE WAKES

MUST BE GLAD

to die before one
wakes
must be glad

(to the same extent
maybe
    that it is also
sad)

a slipping away
in glee
unobserved and
free
in the wide—

area felt spatially,
heart intact.

to die before one
wakes
must be joyous
full swing glorious
(rebellion)
(victory)
unremarked triumph

                              love letters untorn
                              foetal fears
                              unborn
                              monsters given
                              berth

(love unseen, guiltily,
as creation)
                    (life "good")

to die before one
wakes
must be a dance

                              (perhaps a jig)
                              and visual-

skipping tunes of
color
across smirking
eyelids
happy bluely . . .
thought running gaily
out and out.

to die before one
wakes
must be
nice
(green little passions
red dying
into ice
spinningly
   (like a circus)

the blurred landscape
of the runner's
hurried
mile)
one's lips curving
sweetly
in one's most subtle smile.

EXERCISES ON

THEMES FROM LIFE

i

Speaking of death
and decay
It hardly matters
Which
Since both are on the
way, maybe—
to being daffodils.

ii

It is not about that
a poet I knew used
to say
speaking with haunted eyes
of liking and disliking—
Now I think
uncannily
of life.

iii

My nausea has nothing
to do
With the fact that
you love me

It is probably just
something I ate
at your mother's.

iv

To keep up a
passionate courtship
with a tree
one must be
completely mad
In the forest
in the dark one night
I lost my way.

v

If I were a patriot
I would kiss the flag
As it is,
Let us just go.

vi

My father liked very much
the hymns
in church
in the amen corner,
on rainy days
he would wake
himself up
to hear them.

vii

I like to see you try
to worm yourself
away from me
first you plead
your age
as if my young heart
felt any of the tiredness
in your bones . . .

viii

Making our bodies touch
across your breezy bed
how warm you are . . .
cannot we save our little
quarrel
until tomorrow?

ix

My fear of burial
is all tied up with
how used I am
to the spring . . . !

Also of interest:

Alice Walker
Her Blue Body Everything We Know
Earthling Poems 1965–1990 Complete

Pulitzer prize-winning author Alice Walker has been writing
poetry since the summer of 1965. This is the first complete
collection of her work, containing many previously unpublished
poems, plus new introductions to those previously collected.
Bringing valuable new insights and reflections, this beautiful,
definitive volume offers a unique look at a remarkable writer's
development and provides a fascinating retrospective on the
political, social and spiritual issues of the last three decades.

'One cannot read Walker and remain unmoved.' *Books and
Bookmen*

**'One of the most important, grieving, graceful and
honest writers ever to come into print.'** June Jordan

Poetry £9.99/£15.99
ISBN 0 7043 4322 3   Paperback/ISBN 0 7043 5061 0   Hardback

Alice Walker
The Complete Stories

Now in one superb and definitive gift volume come the complete
stories of Alice Walker. Gleaned from her experiences as a child
and young adult in the Deep South, and from her life as an
activist, lover, mother, teacher, wife and friend, this resonant
collection showcases three decades of work from one of the
most gifted writers of our time.

'**Alice Walker conveys the passion, serenity and sense of
freedom that comes from her ability to defy traditions.**'
Essence

'**Alice Walker admirers will yearn to have these on their
shelves.**' *Guardian*

Fiction £15.99
ISBN 0 7043 5066 1

Alice Walker
The Color Purple

Set in the harsh, segregated world of the Deep South, Alice
Walker's compelling and prize-winning novel tells the story of
Celie. Raped by the man she calls father, her two children taken
away from her, and forced into an ugly, loveless marriage, Celie
has no one to talk to but God. Then she meets Shug Avery, singer
and magic woman – and discovers, not the pain of female rivalry,
but the love and support of women.

A massive international bestseller, and winner of the Pulitzer Prize
for Fiction in 1983, *The Color Purple* is also an internationally
successful film, produced by Steven Spielberg.

'Walker's voice has power, poise and conviction.' *Times
Literary Supplement*

'She is one of the most gifted writers of her country.'
Isabel Allende

Fiction £5.99
ISBN 0 7043 3905 6

